TIME!

105 Ways to Get More
Done Every Workday

DAVID COTTRELL

TIME!

105 Ways to Get More Done Every Workday

Inquiries regarding permission for use of the material contained in this book should be addressed to:

CornerStone Leadership Institute
P.O. Box 764087
Dallas, TX 75376
888.789.LEAD

Printed in the United States of America
ISBN: 978-0-9819242-4-3

Credits

Editors	Jeff Morris, Alice Adams
Copy Editor	Kathleen Green, Positively Proofed, Plano, TX info@PositivelyProofed.com
Design, art direction and production	Melissa Monogue, Back Porch Creative, Plano, TX info@BackPorchCreative.com

Contents

INTRODUCTION

Among the aimless you often hear talk about "killing time."
People who are constantly killing time are really killing their own
chances in life. Those who are destined to become successful
are those who make time and use it wisely.

— ARTHUR BRISBANE

How do you save time? You can't. There's no way you can actually save time. If you could, people would be able to put years and years of it in the bank. They would trade, barter and bargain with each other to accumulate as much time as possible… more time than anyone else, and some people – the more miserly among us – would live thousands of years.

But you can't stop time long enough to grab it and put it away, can you? It keeps ticking along at the same speed every day of the year for everybody – rich and poor alike.

So if you don't use every minute that speeds through your existence, time simply winks at you and zips on by, never to be seen again.

When I use the phrase "saving time," what I really mean is using every minute as it comes to you – and using it in some way that benefits you, someone else or all of us.

Thus, as you're reading and you see "save 15 minutes," it actually means that's 15 minutes you can use more wisely to accomplish the next thing on your agenda.

By implementing just one or two tips from this book, you'll likely save at least 12 minutes a day. That's about an hour this week. What if your team could implement four or five tips this week that saved 12 minutes a day? That would save each of them four hours a week. Think things would be a little less stressful and more productive?

Before we go further, I need to make one thing clear – there's nothing magical about these tips, no smoke and mirrors. They're just good, common-sense suggestions that will help you make conscious decisions about how to use your time more wisely and increase your quality of life.

Of course, not every suggestion in this book will apply to you. Just search for one tip that will give you 10, 20, or 30 extra minutes a day. Then find another, and another, and another.

Here is how to get the most out of this book:

- ✦ Read with a highlighter in your hand. Mark keywords or phrases that pertain to your personal situation.

- ✦ Search for the first tip you can use to utilize your time better today! Then, find one or two tips to implement each week. Discuss the tip briefly with your team and ask everyone to try this week's tip. Every environment is different, but chances are, some of these tips will stick with your team and result in exponential time savings for all involved.

✦ Share this book with your spouse, co-workers and friends. The better you become at managing your time, the more time you will have to enjoy each other.

Before you know it, you and your team are achieving more and more every day. Speaking of saving time: What better time to get started than right now?

The bad news is time flies. The good news is you're the pilot.

    – MICHAEL ALTSHULER

TIME!

RISE AND SHINE

The first hour of the morning is the rudder of the day.
— HENRY WARD BEECHER

Your day at the office actually begins before you get there. Each and every day, the kind of day you'll have begins taking shape at home, so get up and get going early! Your day will be more productive if you get going a few minutes earlier than your normal start. Go to bed earlier the night before and set your alarm for a few minutes earlier and you'll discover this one small change may be the best return on your time investment you'll ever make. But, don't stop now. There's more…much more!

Start your morning the night before! You can set the stage for a great, productive day even before you go to sleep. Lay out your clothes, including your shoes (this is important!). Put items needed for work the next day in your car the night before. This may all sound strange, but it will save you time every day – time (before you are thoroughly awake and alert) you would otherwise have to spend thinking, "Now what do

I need to take to work today?"

You can also speed the process by preparing and setting your automatic coffeemaker the night before to provide you with wake-up juice first thing every morning. (Don't have one? Get one!)

 Set your alarm clock 15 minutes ahead. Yes, it's kind of like playing a practical joke on yourself, but you'll be surprised how it can help you get going in the morning if you just wake up and pretend it's 15 minutes later than it actually is. You'll get out the door faster and into the office sooner – or, if some minor catastrophe occurs that throws potholes in your way, you'll have some extra time to wrangle with them.

 If your schedule has some flexibility, arrange to drive to work (and home again in the evening) at off-peak times to miss the rush-hour traffic. The average commuter actually wastes a whopping 90 hours a year or more inching along jam-packed freeways. That's days and days of lost time you could use turning out widgets, writing insurance policies, or roasting hot dogs in the backyard.

 Make each trip to and from the office count for something besides getting to the primary destination. Stop to pick up office supplies, groceries, laundry, or anything else that's on the way. Plan the most efficient route before you even start your car. You'll save time, gasoline and money.

It has been my observation that most people get ahead
during the time that others waste.
– HENRY FORD

GET YOUR ACT TOGETHER

In truth, people can generally make time for what they choose to do;
it is not really the time but the will that is lacking.
— SIR JOHN LUBBOCK

If you've gotten off to a smooth start at home, your day should be ready to cooperate with you by the time you reach your office. Remember, you've already got an extra 15 minutes (unless there was a wreck on the freeway).

It always helps to know where your time is going. So, for the next two weeks, keep track of how you spend your time. Sounds dull, right? Boring, maybe? However, you may discover that you're investing your time in people or things that are not really important to you or your goals. Keep your time log for a short period of time to get a sense of where your time goes so you can make better decisions about how you can better use it.

First order of business: Plan your day. Do this before getting involved in anything – or anyone – else, especially tasks that consume a lot of time, such as answering your e-mail. In just 20 minutes of uninterrrupted time, you can accomplish the same amount of work as you can in 60 minutes of work with interruptions. Is there a better investment of your time?

How you begin your day will determine what you accomplish. If you begin by responding to e-mail, chances are, you'll get sucked into that menacing e-mail vacuum and get nothing else done for hours. Allow time for e-mail in your planning, but responding to the e-mail that arrived overnight is not likely to be your top priority.

Here's how you plan:

(A) **Write down your goals.** These goals can relate to the problems you're working on and the tasks you need to accomplish this day. Make a to-do list. Do your thinking and planning on paper – it minimizes stress and confusion and gives you clarity about the time each item will take. Don't trust your memory. It's too easily confused by stress. Your brain is best used for thinking and creating, not memorizing to-do lists!

(B) **Assign priorities.** Divide your to-do list into A, B, and C priorities. "A" priorities are the activities you believe to be critical for your success today. "B" priorities are important but not critical. "C" priorities are tasks that would be nice to do, but only if you get the time.

(C) **Assign deadlines for the completion of each task or the resolution of each goal or problem.** Give yourself a little extra time to handle the dreaded and inevitable surprises that are hidden in the details.

(D) Allow for the unexpected. Something you don't see coming is going to jump up and demand your attention. Count on it – but don't let these emergencies disrupt the rest of your day. Allow some slack in your schedule for the unexpected. Handle these as quickly as possible. Then get back to work!

(E) Begin with your "A" priorities and work your way to the "nice to do" items. If you accomplish nothing, other than your number one priority, you'll be ahead. One of the worst uses of time is to do your "C" priorities first and never get around to your "A" priorities.

(F) Group similar tasks together. For example, if you can easily accomplish one of your "B" or "C" priorities while dealing with a related "A" priority, go ahead and do it. You'll have all the necessary materials together and can save valuable time not having to refocus for each separate task. Make one trip with two stops, return e-mails at one sitting, return phone calls together, and so forth…while you're "in the groove."

Bonus Timesavers

WHAT ABOUT MULTI-TASKING?

Do you think that doing multiple tasks at the same time is one way you can get more done in less time. Not. Multi-tasking is a great way to do nothing well in a hurry. Granted, if you are multi-tasking trival things, you might knock out two trival things at once. However, if you attempt to multi-task important things, you are asking for trouble. Important things require dedicated focus.

Check out the following wisdom about focus and single-tasking:

- "If you want to make good use of your time, you've got to know what's most important and then give it all you've got."
  – Lee Iacocca

- "To do two things at once is to do neither."
  – Publilius Syrus

- "One cannot manage too many affairs: like pumpkins in the water, one pops up while you try to hold down the other."
  – Chinese Proverb

- "You can't catch one hog when you're chasing two."
  – Moe Schaffer

 Here's one of the most important time savers in this book: Focus on starting tasks rather than finishing them. The greatest challenge is taking the first step – and doesn't it feel good when you finally get rolling? Ah, yes! Even the unpleasant tasks are rarely as bad as you think. Just get started!

 Okay, listen up! Clear your desk…NOW! Despite what some people believe, a cluttered desk does not indicate genius. *Au contraire!* It signals confusion, creates stress and really symbolizes one hot mess. Even mini-clutter will grow and eventually fill every inch.

You've been told since you were a toddler: A place for everything, and everything in its place. Easy to see why, isn't it? How much of your life have you spent – and how much aggravation have you endured – looking for things you or somebody else has misplaced? Searching for your stapler, notepad, or keys is a time-waster and a stress-generator.

Nothing is so fatiguing as the eternal hanging on of an uncompleted task.
– WILLIAM JAMES

CODDLE YOUR COMPUTER

A computer lets you make more mistakes faster than any invention in human history — with the possible exceptions of handguns and tequila.
— MITCH RATCLIFFE

O f all the hi-tech tools in the modern office, the computer is now central. Not only do we now take for granted the access it gives us to a world of information, but it has also become our major tool for thinking, planning, organizing, and communicating. Here are a few tips to avoid wasting valuable time on computer-related problems.

If the top of your desk is cluttered with books, staplers, calculators, and piles of paper, it gets hard to find whatever you need at the moment, doesn't it? It's the same with the most valuable piece of real estate on your desk — your computer screen. Is it cluttered with documents and folders that you last used weeks, months, years ago? Rather than simply glancing at the screen and seeing what you need, do you have to resort to the computer's search function to find a recent file?

That's way too much clutter. Only the documents that are important to you right now should be showing. Everything else should be filed away in well-labeled and well-organized folders and subfolders.

A well-organized computer document file should resemble a good paper filing system – documents grouped in folders, folders grouped within drawers, drawers organized within filing cabinets, cabinets grouped together in file rooms. You can set up the virtual equivalent of a sophisticated physical filing system, and even surpass it in usability and search ability, with a few simple moves on your computer screen.

What about documents you think you must keep but are no longer needed in day-to-day activities? Archive them on external storage media that can be stored outside your office. And whatever method you choose, save your current files hourly or daily, depending on how intensively you're working with them. Nothing wastes time like spending weeks or months re-creating lost work.

Keep your computer running as efficiently as possible.

(A) At regular intervals, or whenever things onscreen seem to be happening in slow motion, run a maintenance application such as Scan Disk or MacTuneUp to clean up your old files and to defragment and reorganize your hard drive. You will immediately see an increase in your computer speed.

(B) Keep up with application and system upgrades; often the new, improved versions work better and are more compatible with other programs.

(C) Do not neglect computer security. Browsing the Web leaves you vulnerable to the scores of new viruses, worms, trojan horses, spyware and adware that crazy people invent to make your life miserable. Download every security update the instant it becomes available. One malicious virus can cost you days of productive time.

Bonus Timesavers

Get Tech Savvy — but Be Reasonable

- **Try out new gadgets.** New electronic wonders are invented almost daily to help you do more in less time. Keep up with the tech pages to see which ones might fit into your work style and lifestyle – to save you time and money, too.

- **Learn about your electronic organizer.** Read – really, read – the instruction manual that came with your PDA. Even better, go to the manufacturer's Web site to find software updates and releases that may boost your productivity. You'll probably find several time-management tools you haven't used.

- **Check your stock portfolio weekly, at the most.** Yes, you can keep up-to-the-minute with your online window into the world of high finance, but is it wise? No, it's just a habit. Unless you're ready to take action, don't waste the time. You'll also suffer a lot less stress and anxiety.

- **Limit your time on Facebook, LinkedIn, Twitter, and such.** Social networking sites are great ways to keep up with your extended network of contacts, but they also extract a huge penalty on your productivity. Pay attention to how much time they take and make sure you're getting a good return on that investment.

- **Bite the bullet: Remove all games from your computer.** After suffering through the inevitable withdrawal, you'll find more productive ways to use computer time…and, believe me, you'll eventually feel a lot better. So what if you didn't make it to level XVIII?

Passwords are an essential part of your computer security, but they can be a pain, can't they? You're supposed to make them impossible for a stranger to guess, yet easy enough for you to remember. Then once you've thoroughly memorized them, you've got to change them every six months (if you follow the experts' recommendations). However, you can keep passwords as simple as possible by mixing up letter-number combinations that seem random but actually reflect information no one else could possibly know.

For instance, when you were 9 years old, back in '73, you had a pet dog named Spike. Here's an easy-to-remember password for you and you alone: 73spike9. Six months from now, change it to 937spike. Here's another tip: You can safely keep all of your passwords, especially the impossible-to-remember ones you use only once or twice a year, on a simple USB plug-in flash drive. Keep it on a key chain with your car keys. That way, when you drive away from the office, you're in total control of your secrets.

To remain productive when you are on the go, sync up you handheld device with your desktop PC each day. That way you have you current calendar, to do's and contacts with you all the time.

The less one has to do, the less time one finds to do it in.
— LORD CHESTERFIELD

Do It Now!

The hardest part of doing anything is the first step. Once you've taken that first step, then all you have to do is keep moving until the job is done. Well, it's a little more complicated than that, but we can agree that getting off dead center, converting inertia into kinetic energy, is the essential thing. As Mark Twain said, "The secret of getting ahead is getting started. The secret of getting started is breaking your complex overwhelming tasks into small manageable tasks, and then starting on the first one."

Seize the day!

Attack procrastination, that nasty habit that can cost you a lot of time, energy and frustration! Putting things off seldom improves the quality of your work. In fact, knowing you have something to do that should already have been done just increases stress. To attack procrastination:

(A) Recognize and admit that procrastination is stealing your time and adding stress to your life.

(B) Write down your goals – you will become more focused on getting the important things done.

(C) Create a to-do list and do it. If there's a task you especially dislike, do it first; as if by magic, it goes away!

(D) Reward yourself every time you complete a task you wanted to delay; this will give you incentive to knock out other unpleasant tasks.

 Clear your inbox daily. That important e-mail that came the other day – or was it last week – that you didn't answer? Well, now it's nagging at you. You've wasted 15 minutes looking for it and still can't find it. You can only hope it wasn't life or death and that the quarter-hour you've lost doesn't keep you from reaching another goal today.

Is there a cure for this? Yes. Develop an "in-today, out-tomorrow" process for all e-mails and paper mail coming into your office. Don't let your inbox pile up – act on it immediately. Don't worry. I guarantee you – more will show up tomorrow!

 Whether you're in your office or away on a business trip, document your expenses as soon as they occur. This keeps you from having to spend time searching for scraps of paper and reconstructing your expenses later. There's even a marvelous new device that you can carry with you on the road – a pocket-size scanner that reads, photocopies, and even records text off of receipts of all shapes and sizes. If you're still using old-tech or low-tech methods, maintain a tally in your organizer and keep the receipts in a pocket file. Either way, submit your receipts and expense report as soon as you get back to the office.

 Be decisive! Being decisive usually means, "Seize the moment!" When someone says to you, "Call me later and we'll set an appointment," respond by saying, "Let's save ourselves a call and make the appointment now."

Then it's done…and you won't have to spend another 15 minutes on a phone call just to arrange a meeting. It seems a lot more sincere, too, doesn't it? "Call me later" is some people's polite way of saying, "I don't really care that much about it."

Never leave 'til tomorrow which you can do today.
— BENJAMIN FRANKLIN

E-MAIL LIKE A PRO

E-mail correspondence is the Whack-the-Mole
game for attention-starved times.
— MITCH THROWER

The era of writing on pieces of paper, sealing them in envelopes, and handing them to a uniformed courier who sends them anywhere in the country in a few days, regardless of the weather, is rapidly drawing to a close. "Snail mail" won't vanish anytime soon, but in the era of instant e-mail and text messaging, it is destined to become a quaint reminder of days gone by. The new standard for delivery is not days but microseconds. A message is dispatched an instant after the last period is typed and — sometimes unfortunately — seen by the recipient an instant after that. It's a terrific timesaver, but a dangerous one, and the sheer ease of using it has vastly increased the volume of written communication, including much that is next to useless and a big waste of time. How can you minimize the time spent dealing with e-mail?

First of all, exercise e-mail discipline. Checking e-mail can become a habit that distracts you from productive work. So, limit checking to two or three times a day. Set a schedule – for example, 9:00 a.m., 1:00 p.m., and 4:00 p.m. If there's anything urgent, respond right away, but be more relaxed about the rest. A true emergency will usually arrive in person or by phone.

Sort your incoming mail by subject or author. This will group related messages that deal with the same or similar subjects and will help you prioritize. This is also a good time to copy new addresses into your e-mail address book. This will save you the frustrating chore of searching through old e-mail to find the address of a person you need to contact again.

Now that you've got them sorted, do one thing immediately with each message: either respond to it, file it for future reference, or delete it. Don't let your inbox be a filing space. It should serve only as a landing strip for incoming e-mail. Respond, file, or delete, but don't leave them in your inbox.

Delete? That's one of the most useful, time-saving keys on your computer keyboard. Use it whenever possible. With e-mail, delete those from people you don't know and have no reason to hear from again. This will save you hours and hours of dealing with spam, viruses, and other annoyances.

Set your e-mail program to filter those you know are spam or other unwanted messages. In addition, delete frivolous e-mail, such as chain letters or the latest list of corny jokes (which you've already seen nine times this month) – even when they're from people you know and like.

Many find it useful to set up a separate e-mail account and give that address to friends who tend to waste their time with junk mail. You can check a "dump" account like this every few days and respond to the few people you don't want to ignore, but whose messages otherwise tend to cut into your productivity.

The Five B's of Sending E-mails:

- **Be Brief** – The longer the e-mail, the less likely it is to be read. Write to the point.

- **Be Clear** – E-mail invokes emotion. Be clear about what emotion you want to deliver – often a call is more effective.

- **Be Simple** – Leave as little to interpretation as possible. The simpler, the better.

- **Be Prompt** – Respond within the expectation of the sender if possible. But never respond before thinking – you can never get your words back!

- **Be Careful** – Anything sent on e-mail is public domain and when you hit the send button, you have no control over where it goes or how it is used.

From *Too Many E-mails* by Tony Jeary

It's easy to get on too many distribution lists – even more so than the old paper memo circuit. If you're on a distribution list for magazines, newsletters, news alerts, or other online materials, review the return-on-your-time investment.

Your best move may be to scroll down to the bottom and unsubscribe. These frequent visitors never go away on their own. Once you're on the list, you're a lifetime member unless you die or opt out. For any periodic, official reports you receive, ask yourself, "Would I pay for this report if I had to?" If not, and if the reports contain nothing you can't do without or find easily through other means, notify the sender and ask to be deleted from the list. If you use only a few lines of a report, ask for a reformat if possible. Getting four pages when you need four lines doesn't make sense, does it?

Do you copy a lot of people when you send or respond to an e-mail message? If so, you may be wasting a lot of people's time – and you may be asking for them to waste more of your time by answering back. When sending an e-mail or writing a memo, distribute only to the people who really need to know.

Sometimes you send an e-mail only to provide information. At other times, you want an answer or some action. When asking for a response from the recipient, always include a "need by" date. This will help the responder prioritize…and it gives you an opening to follow-up with a reminder before the due date.

This approach prevents a lot of miscommunication and saves enormous amounts of time chasing information, appointments, and other business.

He who lets time rule him will live the life of a slave.
– JOHN ARTHORNE

ON THE PHONE

The telephone is still one of the top tools for wasting time, and it's been around long enough to have wasted a millennia of productive time for the population as a whole (just think of how advanced our civilization would be if nobody had to stop to answer the phone!). Nevertheless, it also remains an essential communication tool and one that would be difficult for us to live or conduct business without. The trick is to make it work for you without having it kidnap your workday.

Before you pick up the phone to make a call — and this includes cell phones — organize your thoughts. Write down the topics you want to talk about, information you need to convey, questions you want to ask. This will keep you on track and keep you from having to call back because you forgot something important. In fact, you can eliminate the need for a lot of phone calls by waiting until you've compiled a list of issues you can handle in a single phone conversation – a "talk" file for anyone you call, whether your boss, subordinates, colleagues, even customers. Unless it's a real emergency or if time allows, wait until you have at least two items in the file before calling with your questions. This strategy also may save you a lot of incoming phone calls that might otherwise interrupt your work.

People who are super-organized and who make the best possible use of every minute often schedule their conversations by making telephone appointments hours, days, or even weeks in advance. It's a very orderly system. You prepare by asking the other person to provide (by e-mail or other means) a brief summary of what the conversation will be about. This gives both you and the caller time to prepare for the conversation, perhaps even conduct background research if needed. Callers will appreciate knowing they will have 15 minutes, 30 minutes, or whatever time is available to make a point or get a decision.

It sounds like extra work, but if you invest a few seconds in logging every call you receive, you will be able to tell who calls you the most, how often, and why. Once you see the pattern, negotiate with those who tend to monopolize your time and try to get them to limit the number of calls. Or, ask them to call only on a mutually agreeable schedule. Even if you conduct the same amount of business, handling it in one call is more economical than spreading it out over three or four or five calls.

Caller ID can be a powerful time saver. Using an appropriate voice-mail message, you can ask the caller to describe the issue and how you can help, then promise to return the call. This is a good way to ration your time on the phone without offending callers by putting them on hold or cutting the call short because of other priorities.

 Avoid getting into the habit of talking about the weather as a prelude to talking business. Chatting about the weather wastes more of this nation's productivity than all its bad weather combined. Small-talk relationship building is important in business, but instead of talking about the weather, talk about something personal.

 Want to end the conversation? If you get trapped by a caller who wants to chatter on and on, politely say, "Before we hang up, I need to cover one last point...." Then talk about that point, say "Thanks," and get off the phone.

 Return phone calls at a specified time during the day, preferably during what would otherwise be your least productive time of day – you know, those hours when you tend to be sluggish. It takes little creativity to return calls and answer questions, but talking with someone tends to wake you up and make you more alert, and it's a good way to increase your productivity. However, don't wait until the end of the day unless you really don't want to talk to the person or don't mind getting tied up on the call beyond quitting time.

When you find yourself stuck on Hold, knock out some of those minor tasks from your to-do list. Refill your stamp dispenser or your stapler. Check e-mail. Don't just sit there listening to Kenny G or that commercial about what a caveman could do.

 Stand up when you're on the phone. A USC study found that your brain's information processing speed increases 5 percent to 20 percent when you're standing. Think you may look a little goofy standing around your office? You'd be in good company. Thomas Jefferson, Ernest Hemingway and Winston Churchill all stood while working.

 Invest in a cordless telephone headset. It's amazing how much you can get done if you have both hands free while talking. You can take notes, file papers, sharpen pencils or check e-mail while the caller is rambling. You also can walk across your office to get a book off the shelf or jot down questions that occur to you while the caller is in the middle of a long-winded answer to the previous one.

 When you're driving down the road and your cell phone rings, either ignore it and check your messages when you arrive at your destination, or pull over and park before answering. This will cost you a few minutes, but it will save months of hospital, rehabilitation, and courtroom time. Even with a hands-free phone, your chances of being in an automobile accident greatly increase. In short, phone conversations are dangerous distractions while driving.

Talk does not cook rice.
– CHINESE PROVERB

TALK WITHOUT TALKING

*Lost wealth may be replaced by industry, lost knowledge by study,
lost health by temperance or medicine, but lost time is gone forever.*

— SAMUEL SMILES

Another marvelous, time-saving tool that has also become a
major time waster is voice mail. When it's used correctly, it's
a great way to organize your telephone schedule and defer business
until a more convenient time. When misused, it can become an
obsession, overwhelming your careful daily planning and making
you feel as though you're falling further and further behind. Here's
how to make it work for you:

Limit yourself to checking your voice mail twice a day
only! Log the messages — who, when, what — and
return all of the calls that need answering before you
check your voice mail again. Judge which calls might

better be answered by e-mail or other means. This helps you keep control of your own time, especially when the caller tends to keep you on the phone too long.

 On your voice-mail answering message, state when the person calling may expect you to call back. This eliminates guesswork for the caller and will keep him from calling back two or three times more while you're out.

 Tired of listening to the same boring half-minute of instructions (which you've heard 1,000 times) on someone else's voice-mail system? When you need to leave a message, you can skip the "Hi, you have reached…." message and jump straight to the beep by pressing a special keystroke. Here's the catch – you need to know which phone provider the person you're calling is using. If it's Verizon, press the star (★) key; with Sprint, it's the number 1; for T-Mobile and AT&T, it's the pound (#) key. Good luck guessing…but you can try them all in less time than it takes to listen to the greeting!

 Do you like playing phone tag? Who does? Here's how to stop playing before it starts. When you reach the voice mail of the person you're calling, provide five pieces of information: your name, your phone number, why you called, what you need, and when you're available for a callback. At the end of the message, state your name and number again, slowly and clearly – got that – state your name and number again, slowly and clearly. This makes it easier for the person you called to write them down without having to go back and repeat the message. Then make sure you're by your phone when you said you would be. It's not nice to fool other people into playing this nasty little game.

Now for a more creative use of your voice mail: When you're out of the office and a brilliant idea occurs to you, call your own number and leave yourself a voice mail as a reminder. This technique is also useful when you suddenly remember something you forgot but can be handled when you return. And if you're caught somewhere between planes or taxicabs and don't have a notepad or a PDA handy for note taking, call your voice mail, record your note, and retrieve it whenever you need to by calling and listening to your messages.

Everything comes to him who hustles while he waits.
– THOMAS EDISON

MANAGE YOUR PAPER

We can lick gravity, but sometimes the paperwork is overwhelming.
— WERNHER VON BRAUN

They say today's workplace is becoming paperless because of the myriad of electronic devices we now use to manipulate information. Oh, yeah? Take a tour of the typical workplace these days and see how that's working out. There's still plenty of paper in every office – largely because we have more ways than ever to communicate and to generate information. Because of the leveling of the workplace hierarchy and the empowering of employees, information is being made available to more people than ever. How, then, to tame this anaconda of paper and wrestle it into submission?

If there's one thing that's key to paper management, it is this: Keep it moving! That's simple enough, right? Move the paper in your in-basket to your desktop and see what it's about. Then move it either to a read file, an archive file for historical reference or to your outbox for someone else to handle. Just don't let it pile up in your inbox or become part of an ominously growing mass of paper on your desk. In fact, don't be afraid to put it in that most powerful file of all:

The circular file! That's right…throw things away! Ask yourself, "What's the worst thing that could happen if I throw this away?" Most of the time, you can live with the answer, so start filling that wastebasket! But wait! Does throwing things away give you heartburn? A good general rule is to store potentially useful items for 90 days. Then, re-evaluate their usefulness and either archive them, pass them along to someone who can use them (the office pack rat?), or discard them. Some items need to hit the skids faster. For instance, throw out (or file, or pass along to your dentist) last month's copy of a magazine when this month's copy arrives. Remember, the wastebasket is your friend…find a gigantic one and fill it up!

People who take notes on everything sometimes shoot themselves in the foot by writing bits of information on an assortment of scratch pads, legal tablets, calendars, organizers, sticky notes, and loose fragments of paper. This makes it almost impossible for them to find what they need when they need it…often days or weeks later. Don't become the victim of roving packs of paper scraps. Loose papers and sticky notes tend to vanish.

Keep all your notes in a single place. Name your preference – electronic PDA, spiral-bound notebook or daily planner. Whether you prefer forest products or subatomic particles, choose one and only one place to keep all your notes – telephone numbers, e-mail addresses, Web page URLs, meeting notes, appointments, thoughts while fishing, etc. Keep them organized by date, topic, person –

whatever works best for you. With a PDA or a notebook computer, everything you record is, for all practical purposes, cross-referenced because you can use the "search" function to find items by date, topic or keyword.

If you're in and out of the office, meeting and greeting colleagues, vendors, customers and prospects, you'll probably find dozens of business cards in your pockets and on your desk. Now you've got business to attend to, so what do you do? You open a drawer and dump them all in among the pens and paper clips. This is a good way to frustrate yourself and waste time later when you're trying to get in touch with one of these people.

Instead, enter all the data from the card into your contact database as soon as you sit down at your desk. Then throw away the cards to minimize clutter. This is another of those "do it now" tips that will pay off unimagined dividends in productive time down the road.

Take a good look at your desk and your office. Ask yourself,
"What kind of person works in an environment like that?"
The cleaner and neater your work environment,
the more positive, productive and confident you feel.
— BRIAN TRACY, *Eat That Frog*

GUARD YOUR SPACE

The single greatest killer of your time is other people stealing it.
— ROBERT E. DITTMER

Your office is typically the place where you do most of your thinking, planning, and working. You carefully schedule the appointments of people who want to talk with you so that you can ration visiting time and preserve the rest for working alone. Small wonder, then, that a few interruptions can throw your entire day out of whack and cause you to wonder where the time went. The following tips will help you guard your inner sanctum and keep your workday flowing.

Stay in command of your space by taking the initiative:

✦ When someone drops by your open door unannounced, stand up, walk toward the door, and meet the visitor as he enters — or even outside the door — before he can make his way in. By doing so, you take command of the visit. This tends to limit the length of the interruption because, with everybody standing near the door, nobody can settle in for a long chat.

✦ Don't get trapped into small talk. Immediately ask, "What can I do for you?" This gets the visitor straight to the reason he came to you...or if he has none, it subtly gets him moving along with a minimum of chit-chat.

✦ If your visitor tends to ramble on without any apparent end in sight, be respectful but take control. Signal the end by saying, "One more thing before you go." Then, make your point, pat him on the back, and thank him for stopping by.

✦ If all else fails, begin moving away from your office as if you're on your way to another appointment or the restroom, saying, "Let's discuss this later. Give me a buzz and we'll set an appointment." Then smile, wave, and walk on.

Does the layout of your office invite interruptions? There are ways to make it less drop-in friendly:

    ✦ Arrange your office so your desk doesn't face the door. People are less likely to interrupt if they can't see your face.

✦ Get rid of extra chairs. You can always borrow one from somewhere else if you need it.

✦ Limit pictures on your desk to a special few. The more pictures, the more things for a drop-in visitor to talk about.

✦ Hide your candy dish – it is a major interruption magnet.

Hey, got a minute?" That's a question, not a demand. Don't get angry with the interrupter if you answered, "Sure!" to his question. A better answer would be to take control and say, "Sure. I'll come to your office at noon." In fact, if you get into the habit of scheduling appointments in other people's offices rather than inviting them to your own, you'll have greater control over the length of the meeting.

Henry Ford was always dropping into the offices of his company's executives. When asked why he didn't have them come to his, he replied, "Well, I'll tell you. I've found that I can leave the other fellow's office a lot quicker than I can get him to leave mine."

 Keep track of who's interrupting you, why they are interrupting, and when they interrupt. Chances are, it's mostly your boss. Big surprise, right? If so, sit down with him (in his office, preferably) and see if you can work out a way to minimize these interruptions so you can be more productive.

Here's an example: Schedule one-to-one sessions with him at specified times each week. To prepare for these, keep a log of everything that comes up that you need to discuss with him. Then you can address all the issues in one setting rather than randomly, as they come up. This is an especially useful way to handle interruptions from staff, too.

It's important, however, to emphasize that your door is always open if any employee has something of significance or personal concern to discuss.

It's not so much how busy you are, but why you are busy.
The bee is praised. The mosquito is swatted.
– MARY O'CONNOR

Plan a Meeting

A meeting is an event where minutes are taken and hours wasted.
— James T. Kirk

Any organization requires meetings – in fact, about 11 million business meetings are held every business day. People have to talk about the situation, formulate plans, decide on actions, assign roles, and get motivated before anything can be accomplished collectively.

There's nothing intrinsically wrong with holding a meeting. Then why does the very word "meeting" have such a bad odor? Because it means "a waste of time" in the minds of many who have suffered through innumerable hours of trivia, irrelevancies, false objectives, personal grandstanding, and boredom. As most savvy managers know, a meeting that gets to the point, accomplishes its objectives quickly, and adjourns – in other words, doesn't waste time – can be exciting and invigorating.

Here are some ways to shave meetings to their "lean and mean" essentials:

Is this meeting necessary? That's the first question to answer. Before calling a meeting, make sure it has a purpose. Routine meetings – meetings that occur simply because they happen every Monday at 10:00 a.m. – are not a good investment unless they fulfill – or move forward – your objectives.

Explore meeting alternatives. If you can accomplish objectives by telephone, then save everyone's time and plan a conference call. Make it a personal objective to attend face-to-face meetings less often.

Early morning is usually the best time for any meeting. People are fresher, the challenges of the day have not surfaced, and the odds of everyone arriving on time improve. Meetings after lunch tend to last longer than morning meetings, even with the same agenda and participants.

Here's another tip: Set an offbeat meeting time – instead of 9:30, make it 9:38. People are more likely to remember it. Most people allow extra time when the published time is rounded to the half-hour but will take more care to be prompt when it's at an odd time. Why? It's just one of those sweet mysteries of life.

There should be no "vacationers" at your meeting. Limit the attendance list to only essential people, those who have something to contribute to the meeting's objectives. You're looking for quality, not quantity. Having the right people participate is far more important than getting the maximum number of people in the room. The more people, the longer the meeting lasts.

E-mail each participant the day before the meeting to confirm attendance. Not a good use of your time? Their responsibility? Perhaps, but it wastes a lot more time to keep everybody waiting while you're trying to round up that last person. It's also a good idea, and a good attendance reminder, to distribute advance work for participants. If each person could do research for all the other participants, you can save a significant amount of time for the entire meeting.

At least 24 hours before the meeting, distribute an agenda addressing four important questions:

✦ Why am I investing time in this meeting?

✦ How long will it last?

✦ Who's attending?

✦ What are the expectations?

…And, if you're not the one leading the meeting, ask for an agenda in advance.

Meetings without specific objectives tend to achieve nothing specific. If each person has adequately prepared for the meeting, you will get more done a lot faster!

Make the meeting short! Most managers say at least one-half of their meeting time is wasted. That averages out to 5 hours per week, 250 hours per year for each person involved. Wow! Make it a goal to cut your meeting time in half. If people are prepared before they arrive, most meetings could be accomplished in half the time.

Want to make the meeting as short as possible? Have a stand-up session. Get rid of the chairs and put some podiums in the room. This setting assures everyone will stay awake and will want to get to the point quickly.

Prepare for the unexpected and accommodate the disorganized. Always have extra handouts available. Better to have too many than hold everything up for those last few copies. Make sure you have extra pens and paper to avoid waiting for people who go back to their offices to retrieve supplies.

Our meetings are held to discuss many problems which would never arise if we held fewer meetings.
— Ashleigh Brilliant

Better Meetings

- **Reward truth-telling.** Knowing the truth from the get-go keeps you from having to go back and correct mistakes later. If messengers are shot for telling the truth, they won't show up next time...or if they do, they won't do much talking.

- **Make each meeting unique.** Change the location, time, or room layout. The unexpected has a way of livening up – and speeding up – an otherwise slow and dreary routine.

- **Begin and end each meeting on a positive note** – a recognition of some accomplishment, positive results, good news, words of gratitude, a pleasant surprise. Positive meetings keep people coming back, and on time.

It's been said time and time again, but it still has not gotten through to many people: Turn off your cell phones. A ringing cell phone is more than annoying – it breaks the flow of a meeting, distracts the participants with a side conversation (usually too loud), and it's rude, rude, rude ("I'm a very important person and I've got stuff to do that's more important than this meeting").

One company has effectively killed the cell phone problem by having everyone else in the room stand up and sing "Happy Birthday" at the top of their lungs to anyone whose phone rings. The owner usually doesn't make the same mistake again.

Before everyone arrives, display – on a flip chart, board, or screen – the meeting objectives and scheduled ending time for each objective. Keep focused on what's important and don't allow meeting time for solving hundred-dollar problems when you are spending thousands of dollars on the meeting. Having the objective continuously displayed, along with the time limits, will keep the meeting focused and eliminate the stress of the unknown (Why are we here? How long will this meeting last?) In addition, show when breaks are scheduled so people will not license themselves to leave at their discretion and disrupt your meeting.

 Use the flip chart, board, or display screen to maintain focus on the meeting's direction and to record who is responsible for each action item. Writing on the display will help eliminate confusion. One more thing: Do not speak while you are writing. Wait until you face the audience so you don't have to repeat what you've just said.

The key is not to prioritize what is on the schedule,
but to schedule your priorities.
– STEPHEN COVEY

Run the Meeting

*We can no more afford to spend major time on minor things
than we can to spend minor time on major things.*
— Jim Rohn

If you've done your planning properly, much of the work of keeping the meeting on track already will have been accomplished. What's left is for you to guide the meeting to its successful conclusion, which some managers have likened to "herding cats." With any luck and a few of the following tips, your meeting will go more smoothly and swiftly:

Use a spiral-bound notebook or your laptop computer to capture all meeting notes. Never make notes on loose sheets of paper. This eliminates wasting time searching for what happened at the previous meeting. In fact, your best bet is to use the same device you use for note-taking in your office. Just log your notes in a separate file, labeled with the date and the project or main objective so that it can be accessed easily later.

Bonus Timesavers

Meal Management

- Don't serve breakfast during a meeting. Donuts add to the waistline but have never added to productivity. If breakfast is on the agenda and the meeting starts at 8:38, serve breakfast at 8:00.

- General rule: Don't eat while meeting. If you must continue your meeting during lunch, cover general items that don't require dedicated focus. It's more productive to take a 30-minute lunch break than to try to keep everyone's attention while serving or eating. However, if one of your objectives is social bonding, allocate your mealtime to achieve that objective.

- If eating lunch elsewhere, go at 11:00 or 1:00. You'll spend less time waiting for your food. Going at the same time as everybody else in town will cost you at least 15 minutes.

- If your meeting continues after lunch, do not cater turkey or a heavy menu for lunch. Turkey contains chemicals that are natural sedatives, which is not what you need when everyone needs to be focused and at their best. Ditto a heavy meal. Both can make your meeting slow to a snooze.

61 Focus on what's important. Take care of the most important item on the agenda first. If nothing else is accomplished, make sure you accomplish the most important reason for calling the meeting. This is worth repeating: Do not allow time in meetings for solving hundred-dollar problems when you're spending thousands on the meeting.

Set time limits on how long you will allow people to "sell" their points. Recognize when a decision point has been reached. A lot of meeting time is wasted by people who keep fighting, even after they've lost the battle. This is a good reason for showing the time allotted for each item on the agenda. When the limit has been reached and all views have been expressed at least once, move on to the next item.

If you have someone who is dominating the meeting with his own agenda, hold him to the time limit and assure him that you understand his position. Then, ask him to listen and respect the other participants' points of view so that the group can formulate a course of action.

The only exception is when it's a very crucial or complicated decision being hashed out and more time is obviously needed. Then you need to set a new meeting time and table the issue.

Complete all agenda items before moving to unrelated or non-agenda topics. Put important items not scheduled for the meeting on a "parking lot" flip chart for discussion later. These parking lot issues should be part of the minutes when they are distributed.

Before ending the meeting, create an action plan for the decisions that were made. The meeting is not over until the minutes have been distributed (within two working days) and all action items have been accomplished.

You cannot kill time without injuring eternity.
– HENRY DAVID THOREAU

END THE MEETING

*Sometimes I get the feeling that the two biggest problems
in America today are making ends meet and making meetings end.*
— ROBERT ORBEN

Once the objectives of a meeting have been met, there remains only the graceful exit. The end does not necessarily occur all at once. No, it is often gradual, a slow dawning and then a general recognition that the meeting is, in fact, over. At that point, bang the gavel, pick up your papers, and adjourn.

If it's not important they hear what is scheduled for the rest of the meeting, consider offering participants the option of leaving after they have completed their portion of the meeting. This sends them a signal that their time is valuable, but gives them an opportunity to stay if they feel they can contribute constructively to other matters. By the same token, if you're participating in someone else's meeting, let the meeting leader know in advance that you would prefer to attend only the portion that relates to you. When you've finished your dog-and-pony show, ask if anything further is needed. If not, excuse yourself and go back to your own work.

 Meeting's over. But wait! Do you really think everyone knows what they are supposed to do next? Don't assume anything! Before leaving the meeting, recap so everyone knows who's responsible for any next steps, when action should take place, and how results will be communicated.

 End the meeting on time – or better yet, end early! The minute you go past your stated time, stress levels rise and attention levels fall. Just like school kids, we all enjoy the pleasant surprise of getting out early.

 Never leave a meeting wondering why you went or invested valuable time. If the objectives weren't accomplished, figure out what can be done differently to ensure that the next meeting does not end the same way.

Guard your own spare moments. They are like uncut diamonds.
– RALPH WALDO EMERSON

READY FOR THE ROAD

When preparing to travel, lay out all your clothes and all your money.
Then take half the clothes and twice the money.
— SUSAN HELLER

Business travel remains one of the pleasures — and some times many of the pains — of business. In many ways, it is a major time waster. You're away from the office, where you have your staff and the necessary resources to handle routine tasks and the occasional emergency with superhuman efficiency and cool aplomb (at least that's the way it is around my office). Being on the road, by contrast, is a lot like one long, continuous emergency with only strangers to help you (if they will just listen to reason).

As with everything else, successful travel begins with careful preparation. That's why checklists were invented. But when you travel on business, you not only take part of your home with you…but part of your office as well. For this reason, you need two checklists — one for home and one for the office. Create one for each, laminate them, and keep them in the appropriate places – one in your desk, the other in your travel bag. This will help you double-check the essentials.

Going overseas? Your checklist needs to include your passport, a bank card that can get you instant cash and a cell phone, as well as a computer battery charger and power supply and a cell phone charger that will work where you're going. Check these out carefully on the Web before you go.

You want things to run smoothly back at the office in your absence. Carefully prep your office staff to handle scheduled or expected events as well as contingencies. Ask them to sort your mail and condense it into action items you can handle as soon as you return.

Always carry emergency cash – enough for taxis and tips, and some for "just in case." You don't want to waste time looking for an ATM in an unfamiliar city.

If you haven't already, find an airline, rental car company, and hotel chain you like and stick with them. The more familiar you are with the company, the less time you'll waste learning how they operate, explaining who you are, and getting the best deals. You can save minutes or hours on every trip simply by eliminating the need to fill out redundant information each time you check in.

Don't spend time beating on a wall, hoping to transform it into a door.
– Coco Chanel

Fly Away

There are only two emotions in a plane: boredom and terror.
— ORSON WELLES

Let's get specific about airline travel. These days it's no longer an adventure, except in the sense of surviving its horrors and indignities. And it's no pleasure, unless you or your company are spending premium bucks to put you in big, plush Business or First Class seats with hot-and-cold-running flight attendants.

Worst of all, from the time management perspective, airlines can no longer be relied on to get you or your luggage there on time — or even get you there in time to make your connecting flight. About all you can do is plan your trip to reduce the likelihood of missed connections and be ready for any inconvenience or emergency that occurs…because there's always something.

Join an airline club. The financial investment is easily returned with the work you accomplish when you use their club facilities. You can knock out e-mails, return calls, and relax in a quiet place instead of being in the middle of the action at the gate.

Arrange air travel to avoid making connections in major hubs. Usually, time is wasted waiting for connections. Bad weather or even a computer glitch in another part of the country can cause cascading delays or cancellations at hubs, and even a single late arrival (yours) can mean a missed connection and delays of hours or a full day. Fly point-to-point nonstop when possible, even if it means catching a very early or late flight, renting a car, or catching a bus to complete the trip.

Bonus Timesavers

Working While Waiting

- Create a short-task list – things that can be done in 5, 10, or 20 minutes. Waiting on hold? Knock off some of those 5-minute tasks. What about the others? Most people find 10- to 20-minute gaps in their day – the perfect time to take care of a few more nagging to-do's.

- When you're wasting time waiting in waiting rooms, do you enjoy reading that 3-year-old *People* magazine? I didn't think so. Keep reading materials handy for these occasions. Become a "rip and reader" – scan the magazines that cross your desk and tear out the articles you want to read but don't have time to at that moment. Believe me, their time will come. Print out your e-mails and catch up on them while waiting for a meeting to begin or the plane to start boarding.

- Download podcasts and carry them with you in the car or on the plane for professional training and development during time that would otherwise fly out the window. Use every opportunity to learn.

- If at all possible, don't take the last flight of the day to your destination. If it cancels, you're stuck. Schedule flights to allow yourself get to your destination the same day, even if your original flight is cancelled.

Although it's getting harder to bring carry-on luggage onboard these days, avoid bringing luggage you have to check. Not only will this save you 20 minutes when catching your flight, but it can save 20 minutes or more waiting for it to come down the carousel at the other end. The 20 minutes you save also can put you first in line for a rental car or a cab…and we're not even talking about the days waiting for lost luggage to arrive at your hotel by courier, if it is even found and returned. (Political comic Mark Russell has speculated that the rings of Saturn are made up of lost luggage.)

More than any other item, you can't afford to arrive at your destination without your carefully prepared and rehearsed presentation. Fortunately, there's an easy backup made possible by the miracle of technology: E-mail your presentation to the meeting coordinator ahead of time. Ask someone to load it up and have it ready for you when you arrive. As a backup to your backup, carry the presentation on a keychain flash memory stick just in case something happens to the coordinator's computer.

When traveling internationally, check the movement of the customs lines. Customs agent productivity varies significantly and you can waste a lot of time waiting. Note also that, just as in the grocery store, the shortest lines are not always the fastest. However, unlike the grocery store, fast customs lines tend to remain fast.

How many hours are wasted standing in airplane aisles, bumping your head against the overhead bins, waiting for those ahead of you to fish out their carry-ons and get off the plane? To avoid the worst of this, get an aisle seat as close to the front of the plane as possible. The passengers in the first five rows of a full airplane can usually deplane 10 minutes before those in the back row.

Nothing else you can do? As soon as you get on board, return as many phone calls as you can before the plane leaves the gate and the pilot tells you to shut down your cell phone. But whatever you do, don't say, "Guess where I'm calling from!" It irritates the heck out of other passengers… especially me!

Sometimes you meet really interesting people on a plane and even start excellent friendships. But if you don't have time or are not inclined to socialize during the flight, invest in a good pair of white-noise headphones. These neutralize almost all the noise on the plane (read "screaming babies") and most people will understand that you don't want to engage in conversation. If this doesn't work, smile and politely tell the talkative person next to you that you've got work to complete before you land. That should be enough to inspire courtesy and silence from your seatmate.

Now you're off your plane and have checked into your hotel. If you're smart, you'll have booked a room on one of the lower floors so you don't have to wait for an elevator but can keep your running muscles toned by using the stairs. It's like getting a seat near the front of the airplane, but with a lot more exercise.

Also, request a room away from the ice machine or elevator. You can lose a lot of sleep when the "team" arrives to fill up their ice buckets at 3:00 in the morning.

Never let yesterday use up today.
– Richard H. Nelson

TAKE THE WHEEL

Time = life; therefore, waste your time and waste of your life,
or master your time and master your life.
— ALAN LAKEIN

At least part of every business trip involves an automobile – sometimes a cab – but more often a rental or company car. Everybody knows how to drive, right? Well, some of the time you wasted in cars – which for most people turns out to be a substantial fraction of their lives – can be regained if you know how to work the system. Here's how:

When scheduling car trips into or out of a city, time your arrivals and departures during off-peak traffic hours. If this is impossible, then travel into the city center during the afternoon traffic or out of the city in the morning, when most traffic is going the opposite direction. This is the only known situation in which going "against the flow" is the fastest way to get where you want to go.

Join a rental car "preferred" club. You'll eliminate the stress of standing in line at the airport – and you can save at least 15 minutes on every rental.

Rent a car with a GPS device. If GPS is not available, log onto the Internet before leaving the office and get directions from the airport to your destination. These maps are usually more reliable and more understandable than directions you get from the rental car counter. Your smart phone may also have GPS built in and can guide you with an on-screen map.

When driving to any location for the first time, use the incredible power of the Internet to prepare for the trip. Look up the location on MapQuest or Google, then zoom in. Look for nearby freeway exits, street intersections, large buildings, parks, and other easy-to-recognize landmarks. Switch to street view and see what your destination will look like when you drive up. A few minutes of "rehearsal" may save you an hour of driving around...and the frustration of being "lost."

Isn't it funny how your car sometimes plays tricks on you by moving while you're gone? As soon as you park, whether in an airport parking lot or a garage downtown, write down your car's exact location in your electronic or paper organizer. If it's a rental car, write down the make and color, and perhaps the license plate. Believe me, it's easy to forget what kind of car you have this trip (or was it the last trip?). This can save you untold time and stress, frantically searching through acres of other people's cars.

Don't let your gas tank get below half-full. If it gets low in unfamiliar territory, you may spend a lot of time anxiously looking for a gas station. Back at home, you'll always save time by filling your gas tank on the way home from work rather than wasting your prime morning time at the pump.

*Those who make the worst use of their time
are the first to complain of its shortness.*
— JEAN DE LA BRUYERE

COVERING THE BASICS

Unlike other resources, time cannot be bought or sold, borrowed or stolen, stocked up or saved, manufactured, reproduced, or modified. All we can do is make use of it. And whether we used it or not, it nevertheless slips away.
— JEAN-LOUIS SERVAN-SCHREIBER

A lot of what constitutes good time management comes down to basic principles – the philosophy and mindset you apply to everyday life in the office and at home. Here are some important reminders of how valuable your time is and how you can bank that value:

Choose and use only one time management system. Whether you choose an electronic or paper system, one consistent system will eliminate much wasted time spent searching for information. Find the system that fits you best and stick with it.

According to the Pareto Principle, 80 percent of your results will come from 20 percent of your activities. Want to be more efficient? Figure out the 20 percent that are your most important activities and spend your time mastering those activities.

 Don't let the perfect be the enemy of the good. "Perfection paralysis" is expensive. Sometimes it is not worth the effort to make things perfect. Take a look at time costs involved and weigh these against the benefit of perfection. Many times second-best in motion is better than first-best still on the drawing board.

 Work smarter, not harder. One of the worst things you can do is something really well that shouldn't have been done at all. Doing inefficient things more diligently does nothing but wear you out faster. Figure out ways to shorten tasks by eliminating steps, combining parts, and getting more done by working easier.

 Know your organization. Take time to understand the role of every department. Investing this time up-front will give you more confidence and better grounding when someone from outside your department comes to you with an urgent request.

 When confronted with a request for help, never say "yes" without considering the time investment. Having the courage to say "no" to requests that are inappropriate or unnecessary could be your most effective time management tool.

Sure, sometimes it's great to be able to help…and it's good to be considered the go-to person in any organization. Just remember to keep your primary responsibilities uppermost and use your time effectively to accomplish your own objectives first.

 Is it your job to pick up every ball that someone drops? I surely hope not. It's not up to you to solve everyone else's problems. Be empathetic to another's situation, but if you spend your time solving their problems, surprise! Their next problem will become yours, too! The best thing you can do is help others learn how to solve their own problems.

 Want to make a positive difference? Ask your peers and subordinates, "What do I do that wastes your time and hinders your performance?" Be prepared for some frank – and surprising – answers. You may learn that some of your efforts are not really helping others be more productive.

 Continually ask yourself the number one time management question of all time: ***What's the best use of my time right now?***

 Give yourself a break and create a quiet time for planning. You can accomplish 60 minutes' worth of interrupted work in just 20 minutes of uninterrupted time. Is there a better investment of your time? Let everyone know that your closed door means "do not disturb" unless there is an emergency – or someone in your family calls.

Pay attention to your daily biorhythms. Discover your personal peak times and use your energy accordingly. Take on creative projects when you are the sharpest... and do the mundane stuff when you're least creative. Not everybody is a morning person!

 Create "mental space" to clear your mind of distractions. Turn off your car radio, give your ears a rest and that can help clear your mind. At home, turn off your computer, television, and music. Spend some time in quiet mediatition. Look around – enjoy the nature.

Taking time to clear your mind will re-boot your energy and attitude.

You can't turn back the clock. But, you can wind it up again.
— BONNIE PRUDDEN

BACK HOME

All intellectual improvement arises from leisure.
— SAMUEL JOHNSON

---

101 Rest. The more rested you are, the more you can accomplish when you work. If you're tired, you work slower, make more mistakes, and fail to see obvious solutions. Avoid taking work home for the weekend if possible. Guard your health. If you burn out, you're not doing yourself, your job, or your family any favors. Work hard and efficiently, but try to leave your work at the office.

102 Worried about something? Do something about it! Worry robs us all of time and energy. Sure, it's natural to worry, but you can shorten the time between when you start worrying and when you begin doing something about it.

Turn off the television! Watching television is a habit. Enjoy your favorite programs, but turn the television off when you are just veggin' in front of the plasma. If you DVR your favorites, you'll save 20 minutes of every hour in front of the television by fast-forwarding through the commercials.

Now that you have the time, read something positive. If you will read something positive 10 minutes a day, it can change your outlook on life.

Get involved in activities outside of work. The more you help others, the better you will feel about yourself and your job. There are plenty of people who could use your encouragement today – try it.

Bonus!

Give a copy of this book to your spouse, co-workers and friends. The better you become at managing your time, the more time you will have to enjoy each other.

Don't say you don't have enough time. You have exactly the same number of hours per day that were given to Helen Keller, Pasteur, Michelangelo, Mother Teresa, Leonardo da Vinci, Thomas Jefferson, and Albert Einstein.
    – H. JACKSON BROWN

ABOUT THE AUTHOR

David Cottrell, president and CEO of CornerStone Leadership Institute, is an internationally known leadership consultant, educator, and speaker. His business experience includes leadership positions with Xerox and FedEx. He also led the successful turnaround of a Chapter 11 company before founding CornerStone in 1996.

David is a thought-provoking and electrifying professional speaker. His most popular topics are *Monday Morning Leadership, Monday Morning Choices* and *Monday Morning Motivation.* He has presented his leadership message to over 300,000 managers worldwide.

To invite David to speak at your next leadership conference, please contact Michele@CornerStoneLeadership.com.

David and his wife, Karen, reside in Horseshoe Bay, Texas. He can be reached at www.**CornerStoneLeadership**.com

Also by David Cottrell

136 Effective Presentation Tips

Birdies, Pars, and Bogeys: Leadership Lessons from the Links

David Cottrell's Collection of Favorite Quotations

Becoming the Obvious Choice

Escape from Management Land: A Journey Every Team Wants Their Leader to Take

Listen Up, Customer Service

Listen Up, Leader

Listen Up, Teacher

Leadership … Biblically Speaking

Leadership Courage

Management Insights

Monday Morning Choices

Monday Morning Communications

Monday Morning Customer Service

Monday Morning Leadership

Monday Morning Mentoring

Monday Morning Motivation

The Leadership Secrets of Santa Claus

The Manager's Coaching Handbook

The Manager's Communication Handbook

The Manager's Conflict Resolution Handbook

The Nature of Excellence

The Next Level: Leading Beyond the Status Quo

Winners Always Quit! Seven Pretty Good Habits You Can Swap for Really Great Results

www.CornerStoneLeadership.com

Accelerate Personal Growth Package
$179.95

Order Form

1-30 copies $12.95   31-50 copies $11.95   51-99 copies $10.95   100+ copies $9.95

TIME!   _____ copies X _____   = $ _____

Additional Personal Development Resources

Accelerate Personal Growth Package   _____ pack(s) X $179.95   = $ _____
 (Includes all items pictured on previous page.)

Other Books

_____   _____ copies X _____   = $ _____

_____   _____ copies X _____   = $ _____

_____   _____ copies X _____   = $ _____

_____   _____ copies X _____   = $ _____

_____   _____ copies X _____   = $ _____

                                     Shipping & Handling $ _____

                                     Subtotal $ _____

                                     Sales Tax (8.25%-TX Only) $ _____

                                     Total (U.S. Dollars Only) $ _____

Shipping and Handling Charges

Total $ Amount	Up to $49	$50-$99	$100-$249	$250-$1199	$1200-$2999	$3000+
Charge	$7	$9	$16	$30	$80	$125

Name _____ Job Title _____

Organization _____ Phone _____

Shipping Address _____ Fax _____

Billing Address _____ E-mail _____

City _____ State _____ ZIP _____

❏ Please invoice (Orders over $200) Purchase Order Number (if applicable) _____

Charge Your Order: ❏ MasterCard   ❏ Visa   ❏ American Express

Credit Card Number _____ Exp. Date _____

Signature _____

❏ Check Enclosed (Payable to: CornerStone Leadership)

Fax	**Mail**	**Phone**
972.274.2884	P.O. Box 764087	888.789.5323
	Dallas, TX 75376	

www.**CornerStoneLeadership**.com

Thank you for reading *TIME!*
We hope it has assisted you in your quest for
personal and professional growth.

CornerStone Leadership is committed to providing new
and enlightening products to organizations worldwide.
Our mission is to fuel knowledge with practical resources
that will accelerate your team's productivity,
success and job satisfaction!

Best wishes for your continued success.

CornerStone
Leadership Institute
www.CornerStoneLeadership.com

Start a crusade in your organization –
have the courage to learn, the vision to lead,
and the passion to share.